POINTS OF VIEW

Should the United States HELP OTHER COUNTRIES?

By Maya Morrison

KidHaven PUBLISHING

Published in 2022 by
KidHaven Publishing, an Imprint of Greenhaven Publishing, LLC
353 3rd Avenue
Suite 255
New York, NY 10010

Designer: Deanna Paternostro
Editor: Caitie McAneney

Photo credits: Cover Stocktrek Images/Stocktrek Images/Getty Images; p. 5 Mikael Vaisanen/The Image Bank/Getty Images; p. 7 Handout/Handout/Getty Images News/Getty Images; p. 9 (main) ZOOM DOSSO/Stringer/AFP/Getty Images; p. 9 (inset) NurPhoto/Contributor/NurPhoto/Getty Images; p. 11 Robert Alexander/Contributor/Archive Photos/Getty Images; p. 13 ORLANDO SIERRA/Contributor/AFP/Getty Images; p. 15 Scott Olson/Staff/Getty Images News/Getty Images; p. 17 Barcroft Media/Contributor/Barcroft Media/Getty Images; p. 19 Thomas Imo/Contributor/Photothek/Getty Images; p. 21 (notepad) ESB Professional/Shutterstock.com; p. 21 (markers) Kucher Serhii/Shutterstock.com; p. 21 (photo frame) FARBAI/iStock/Thinkstock; p. 21 (inset, left) U.S. Navy/Handout/Getty Images News/Getty Images; p. 21 (inset, middle) MARWAN IBRAHIM/Stringer/AFP/Getty Images; p. 21 (inset, right) Jacob Maentz/The Image Bank Unreleased/Getty Images.

Library of Congress Cataloging-in-Publication Data

Names: Morrison, Maya, author.
Title: Should the United States help other countries? / Maya Morrison.
Description: New York : KidHaven Publishing, [2022] | Series: Points of view | Includes index.
Identifiers: LCCN 2020030807 | ISBN 9781534536555 (library binding) | ISBN 9781534536531 (paperback) | ISBN 9781534536548 (set) | ISBN 9781534536562 (ebook)
Subjects: LCSH: Economic assistance–United States–Juvenile literature. | Debates and debating–United States–Juvenile literature.
Classification: LCC HC60 .M614 2022 | DDC 327.1/11–dc23
LC record available at https://lccn.loc.gov/2020030807

Printed in the United States of America

CPSIA compliance information: Batch #CS22KH: For further information contact Greenhaven Publishing LLC, New York, New York at 1-844-317-7404.

CONTENTS

A World LEADER

For many years, the United States has been seen as a world leader. In fact, most people around the world see it as the world's top **economic** power. The United States makes more money than any other country. It also gives money and help to many countries in need.

Some people believe the United States has a duty to help other countries. They think it has enough money to go around and that helping others is the right thing to do. Other people think the United States gives too much to other countries.

Know the Facts!

A 2018 Pew Research survey found that across 25 countries, about 39 percent of people saw the United States as the world's leading power—a greater number than thought that of China, the European Union (EU), or Japan.

Should the United States help other countries? Let's look at both sides of this debate, or argument.

How Do We HELP?

The United States gives aid to many countries who need help. This is called foreign aid, and it can be money, help in the form of people, or materials. The United States may help set up **infrastructure** in a country, provide important medicines and food supplies, or help a group defend itself from harm.

Sometimes, a natural or man-made **disaster** hits a country, and the United States steps in to help. One U.S. government office, USAID, helps with about 65 disasters in 50 countries each year. The office gives food, water, and supplies to people affected by storms, earthquakes, **famines**, and war.

Know the Facts!

According to USAID, in just over 10 years, the number of people in need of humanitarian aid has more than doubled.

Much of foreign aid is considered humanitarian aid. "Humanitarian" means having concern for the welfare, or wellness, of other people.

Saving LIVES

Many people argue that the United States has the ability and the duty to save lives around the world. Over the past three decades, U.S. foreign aid has helped reduce the number of people living in extreme, or serious, **poverty** from 36 percent to 8 percent of the world's population. The death rates for mothers, babies, and children have been cut in half. People around the world are living longer. Many deadly illnesses have been almost wiped out in many countries, thanks to U.S. aid.

U.S. aid can keep diseases, or illnesses, from spreading. For example, U.S. aid helped stop the spread of a deadly disease called Ebola in Africa.

Know the Facts!

In only five years, a program led by the United States that gave vitamin A to children in Nepal cut the death rate for children under five in half in that country.

People who believe the United States should help other countries believe U.S. aid can save lives in parts of the world such as Nepal (left) and Africa (above).

Too Much MONEY

Foreign aid programs often cost a lot of money. Some people argue that these programs cost too much. Some also say that it's not fair that the United States spends more than any other country on foreign aid. They say that other countries should be stepping up more to help.

Some Americans believe this money could be better spent within the United States. They point to people living in poverty in this country. Americans living in poverty struggle to afford housing, food, and health care.

Know the Facts!

In 2019, the U.S. budget, or spending plan, included $39.2 billion for foreign aid.

Some U.S. veterans, or people who served in the military, don't have services they need. About 50,000 veterans are homeless. Some people say foreign aid money should go to help U.S. veterans instead.

A Small Price TO PAY

Some people say that providing aid is a small price to pay for the United States to promote, or support, global peace and welfare. While the United States planned to spend about $39.2 billion on foreign aid in 2019, that was less than 1 percent of the country's budget. While the United States provides more foreign aid than other countries, it's a smaller portion of its income than what comes from most other wealthy nations.

Foreign aid can make a huge difference in the **development** of other countries. That can help people stay in their home countries instead of moving to other places as **refugees**.

Know the Facts!

Opinion polls have shown that many Americans believe foreign aid takes up about 25 percent of the nation's spending. The amount is actually less than 1 percent.

USAID helped deliver testing kits to countries such as Honduras during the COVID-19 **pandemic**. This helped keep people safe in that country and around the world.

Not a SOLUTION

Americans who oppose giving foreign aid say that this aid doesn't solve, or fix, problems. They say that some countries still have poor economies, even when the United States has helped them for a long time. They believe that foreign aid makes those countries needy instead of better able to help themselves.

Some believe the United States shouldn't get involved in another country's conflicts, or fighting. U.S. troops have spent nearly 20 years in Iraq and Afghanistan as part of the "War on Terror," meant to fight **terrorism** in the Middle East. This has cost the United States more than $975 billion and thousands of U.S. lives.

Know the Facts!

A 2019 Pew Research poll found that 58 percent of U.S. veterans and 59 percent of U.S. citizens believed that United States involvement in Afghanistan wasn't worth it.

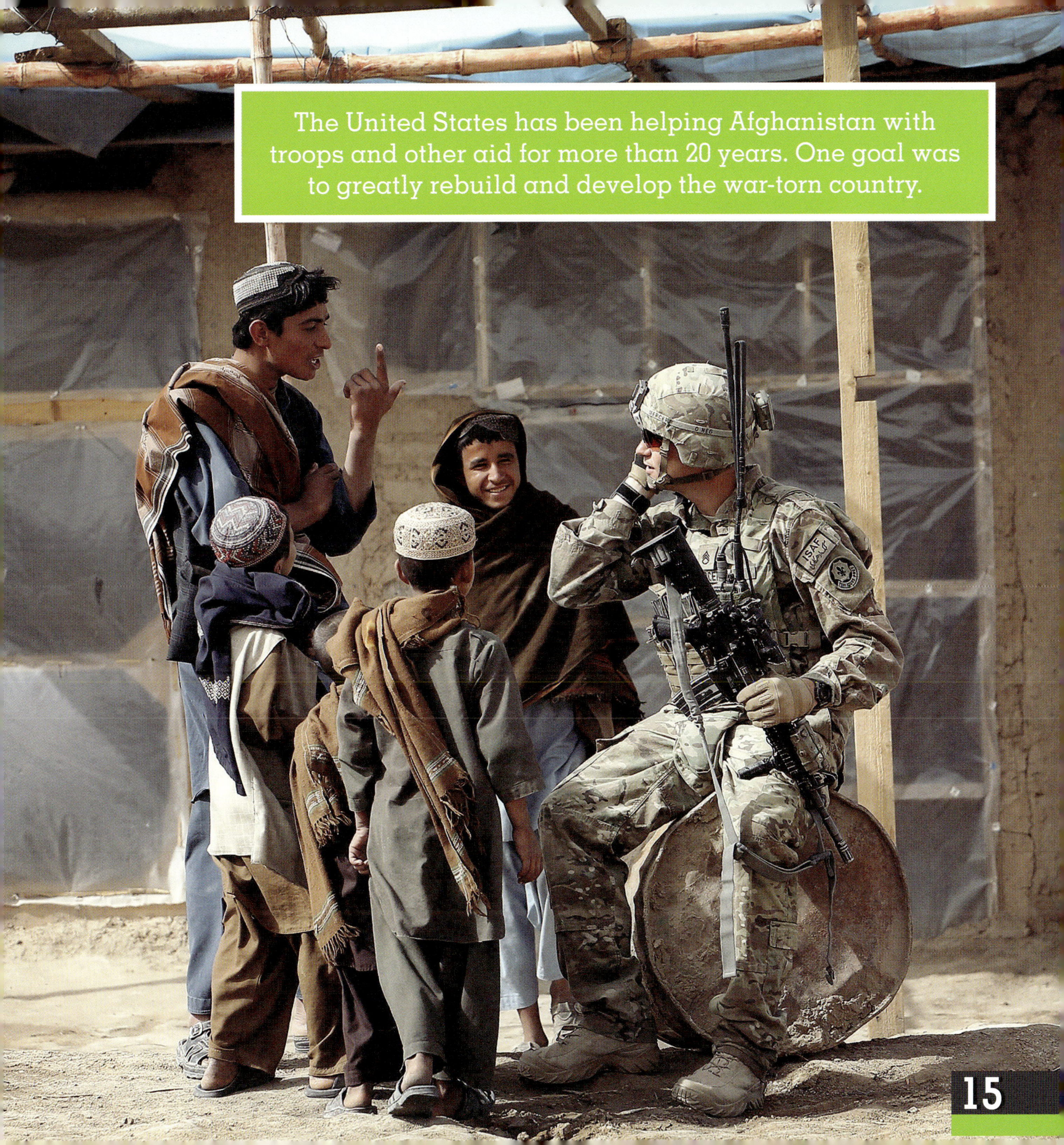

The United States has been helping Afghanistan with troops and other aid for more than 20 years. One goal was to greatly rebuild and develop the war-torn country.

Promoting PEACE

Some people argue that sending aid to other countries can promote peace. Supporting allies, or partner countries, in their times of struggle can be good for the world. It can increase global, or worldwide, **security** and promote world peace.

The United States has been active in trying to keep terrorist groups and unjust governments from harming countries around the world. In 2000, the United States and Colombia (in South America) started working together to fight **rebel** groups. U.S. foreign aid helped Colombia work toward peace and rebuild the nation after war.

Know the Facts!

The United States often helps its allies fight for **democracy**, which can help other nations' **stability**. Said Djinnit, a United Nations representative for West Africa, said during a 2010 interview, "Stability, long-lasting stability, is based on democracy."

The United States often helps people who are stuck in war zones. This U.S. soldier is talking to young people in war-torn Syria.

The Wrong HANDS

What if U.S. aid falls into the wrong hands? This can happen. Sometimes it is used by corrupt, or dishonest and greedy, leaders. Some people argue that giving aid to countries that might have corrupt people handling it is a waste.

The U.S. government has given foreign aid to African countries to fight malaria—a deadly sickness spread by mosquitoes. However, millions of dollars worth of malaria medicine has been stolen and resold unlawfully. Leaders of some other countries have taken U.S. aid without using it for the people who really need it.

Know the Facts!

In 2017, a South African doctor pled guilty to stealing more than $200,000 in U.S. funds meant to help promote safer childbirth practices in South Africa.

U.S. money helps prevent, or stop, malaria in African countries. It pays for medicine and ways to keep people safe from mosquitoes. In 2018, there were about 228 million malaria cases and 405,000 deaths worldwide.

A Strong NATION

Should the United States give money and help to other countries? Does U.S. foreign aid make a difference in the world?

Some people think giving foreign aid makes the United States a strong world leader. It helps to uphold peace in the world. They say it's the duty of a wealthy nation to take care of other nations. Others think U.S. money and lives shouldn't be spent helping others when there are problems to solve within the United States. There are many strong arguments on both sides of this debate!

Know the Facts!

A Pew Research poll found that a growing number of Americans say the United States should be active in world affairs, or events.

Should the United States help other countries?

YES

- The United States has a duty to help other countries, especially with humanitarian issues.
- Foreign aid can save lives through important medicine and food supplies.
- Foreign aid is less than 1 percent of the U.S. budget—a small price that makes a big difference.
- Helping other countries in their conflicts can promote peace and democracy in those countries and around the world.

NO

- The United States spends too much money on other countries.
- The United States could be spending foreign aid money to help its own citizens.
- Foreign aid doesn't solve problems and may cause other countries to become needy.
- Foreign aid money can fall into the wrong hands and be used in corrupt ways.

Look at arguments and facts to help make your own informed, or educated, opinion!

GLOSSARY

democracy: A government elected by the people, directly or indirectly.

development: The act or process of growing or causing something to grow.

disaster: Something that happens suddenly and causes much suffering and loss for many people.

economic: Having to do with the way things are made, sold, and used in a country or area.

famine: A situation in which many people do not have enough to eat.

infrastructure: The basic equipment and structures that are needed for a country, region, or organization to function properly.

pandemic: An outbreak of disease that occurs over a wide geographic area and affects a great proportion of the population.

poverty: The state of being poor.

rebel: Having to do with those who fight against authority or try to overthrow a government.

refugee: Someone who is seeking a safe place to live, especially during a time of war.

security: The state of being safe.

stability: The quality of being peaceful, safe, or steady.

terrorism: The use of violence and fear as a way to achieve a political goal.

For More INFORMATION

WEBSITES

11 Facts About Global Poverty
www.dosomething.org/us/facts/11-facts-about-global-poverty
Learn more about how poverty affects people around the world.

War in Afghanistan
www.ducksters.com/history/us_1900s/war_in_afghanistan.php
Explore more facts about U.S. involvement in Afghanistan.

BOOKS

DK. *People and Places: A Visual Encyclopedia*. New York, NY: DK Publishing, 2019.

Donaldson, Olivia. *Malaria (Deadliest Diseases of All Time)*. New York, NY: Cavendish Square, 2015.

Roberts, Ceri, and Hanane Kai. *Refugees and Migrants*. London, UK: Wayland Publishing, 2018.

INDEX